Joseph: a Man of Integrity
Pictures

General Church
Office of Education

These pictures can be used independently or as part of the *Joseph: A Man of Integrity* series of lessons for ages 3-18. For more information on this series, visit **www.newchurch.org/youth-journey-programs**.

You can also find us on Facebook (**facebook.com/NewChurchSundaySchools**) and on YouTube (**youtube.com/ncsundayschools**).

The weaving shown on the cover was hand created by Dinah Rose. The General Church Office of Education is grateful for her kindness in letting us photograph and use this piece. For more information about her weaving and to see other pieces, visit **www.dinahrose.com**.

Cover photograph and design by Douglas Keith

Printed in the United States of America.
ISBN 9780945003601
Library of Congress Control Number 2012948797

Copyright © 2012
General Church of the New Jerusalem
Office of Education
Bryn Athyn, PA 19009

REVERSE: Joseph is his father Jacob's favorite child.
See Genesis 37:3.

Use with Lesson 1 of Joseph: A Man of Integrity

Artist: Marguerite L. Acton
© 2012 General Church of the New Jerusalem
1100 Cathedral Road
Bryn Athyn, PA 19009

REVERSE: Joseph is given a coat of many colors by his father, Jacob. See Genesis 37:3.

Use with Lesson 1 of Joseph: A Man of Integrity

Artist: Marguerite L. Acton
© 2012 General Church of the New Jerusalem
1100 Cathedral Road
Bryn Athyn, PA 19009

REVERSE: Joseph dreams of sheaves of grain.
See Genesis 37:5-8.

Use with Lesson 1 of Joseph: A Man of Integrity

Artist: Marguerite L. Acton
© 2012 General Church of the New Jerusalem
1100 Cathedral Road
Bryn Athyn, PA 19009

REVERSE: Joseph dreams of the sun, moon, and stars.
See Genesis 37:9-11.

Use with Lesson 1 of Joseph: A Man of Integrity

Artist: Marguerite L. Acton
© 2012 General Church of the New Jerusalem
1100 Cathedral Road
Bryn Athyn, PA 19009

REVERSE: Joseph is cast into a pit and sold into slavery.
See Genesis 37:23-28.

Use with Lesson 1 or 2 of Joseph: A Man of Integrity

Artist: Marguerite L. Acton
© 2012 General Church of the New Jerusalem
1100 Cathedral Road
Bryn Athyn, PA 19009

REVERSE: Joseph is thrown into prison in Egypt for something he did not do. See Genesis 39:1-20.

Use with Lesson 2 of Joseph: A Man of Integrity

Artist: Marguerite L. Acton
© 2012 General Church of the New Jerusalem
1100 Cathedral Road
Bryn Athyn, PA 19009

REVERSE: The Baker dreams of the bread being eaten by birds.
See Genesis 40:16-19.

Use with Lesson 2 of Joseph: A Man of Integrity

Artist: Marguerite L. Acton
© 2012 General Church of the New Jerusalem
1100 Cathedral Road
Bryn Athyn, PA 19009

REVERSE: The Butler is restored to his position and serves Pharaoh.
See Genesis 40:21.

Use with Lesson 2 of Joseph: A Man of Integrity

Artist: Marguerite L. Acton
© 2012 General Church of the New Jerusalem
1100 Cathedral Road
Bryn Athyn, PA 19009

REVERSE: Pharaoh dreams of seven fat cows and seven gaunt cows. See Genesis 41:1-4.

Use with Lesson 3 of Joseph: A Man of Integrity

Artist: Marguerite L. Acton
© 2012 General Church of the New Jerusalem
1100 Cathedral Road
Bryn Athyn, PA 19009

REVERSE: Pharaoh dreams of seven plump stalks of grain
and seven thin stalks of grain.
See Genesis 41:5-7.

Use with Lesson 3 of Joseph: A Man of Integrity

Artist: Marguerite L. Acton
© 2012 General Church of the New Jerusalem
1100 Cathedral Road
Bryn Athyn, PA 19009

REVERSE: Joseph interprets Pharaoh's dreams and advises him on what to do.
See Genesis 41:25-36.

Use with Lesson 3 of Joseph: A Man of Integrity

Artist: Marguerite L. Acton
© 2012 General Church of the New Jerusalem
1100 Cathedral Road
Bryn Athyn, PA 19009

REVERSE: Grain is gathered up in Egypt during seven years of plenty.
See Genesis 41:47-49.

Use with Lesson 3 of Joseph: A Man of Integrity

Artist: Marguerite L. Acton
© 2012 General Church of the New Jerusalem
1100 Cathedral Road
Bryn Athyn, PA 19009

REVERSE: Joseph has grain stored up in Egypt in preparation for the famine. See Genesis 41:47-49.

Use with Lesson 3 of Joseph: A Man of Integrity

Artist: Marguerite L. Acton
© 2012 General Church of the New Jerusalem
1100 Cathedral Road
Bryn Athyn, PA 19009

REVERSE: Joseph's brothers come before him to buy grain.
See Genesis 42:5-8.

Use with Lesson 4 of Joseph: A Man of Integrity

Artist: Marguerite L. Acton
© 2012 General Church of the New Jerusalem
1100 Cathedral Road
Bryn Athyn, PA 19009

REVERSE: Joseph weeps in private after seeing his brother Benjamin.
See Genesis 43:29-30.

Use with Lesson 5 of Joseph: A Man of Integrity

Artist: Fay S. Lindrooth
© 2012 General Church of the New Jerusalem
1100 Cathedral Road
Bryn Athyn, PA 19009

REVERSE: Joseph's cup is found in Benjamin's sack.
See Genesis 44:11-12.

Use with Lesson 5 of Joseph: A Man of Integrity

Artist: Fay S. Lindrooth
© 2012 General Church of the New Jerusalem
1100 Cathedral Road
Bryn Athyn, PA 19009

REVERSE: Joseph reveals his identity to his brothers.
See Genesis 45:3-8.

Use with Lesson 6 of Joseph: A Man of Integrity

Artist: Marguerite L. Acton
© 2012 General Church of the New Jerusalem
1100 Cathedral Road
Bryn Athyn, PA 19009

REVERSE: Joseph's brothers bring their family and flocks to Egypt.
See Genesis 46:5-7.

Use with Lesson 7 of Joseph: A Man of Integrity

Artist: Marguerite L. Acton
© 2012 General Church of the New Jerusalem
1100 Cathedral Road
Bryn Athyn, PA 19009

REVERSE: Jacob with sons and grandsons in Egypt.
See Genesis 47:11-12.

Use with Lesson 7 of Joseph: A Man of Integrity

Artist: Marguerite L. Acton
© 2012 General Church of the New Jerusalem
1100 Cathedral Road
Bryn Athyn, PA 19009

www.ingramcontent.com/pod-product-compliance
Lightning Source LLC
Chambersburg PA
CBHW040057160426
43192CB00002B/97